Glass Half Hopeful

Library of Congress Control Number: 2023914030

ISBN (paperback): 979-8-9884759-0-3

First Edition: August 2023

For: Cinia,
my little muse

"We do not read and write poetry because it's cute. We read and write poetry because we are members of the human race, and the human race is filled with passion."

- Walt Whitman

Contents

Humbling

Minimum Wage

I'm a part-time poet.
I only work half hours,
half days or weeks,
even years.
Partially there and partially here.
My words are not contract based,
you cannot give them a time,
nor a date.
They flow out during a moment,
in the midst of a memory being made.
They hold no boundaries,
show no grace.
A part-time job,
yet ever consuming.
Thc only reason I keep it
is so my words can't ruin me.

The House That Built Me

I've lived in half-finished homes my whole life.
The walls were never quite painted enough.
The furniture was never completely moved in.
The decorations never fully made it out of the boxes.
Still, without all of that,
I never missed a moment.
I clung to every memory made in those half houses.
Because even with the missing molding
and blinds that never shut tight.
Those places grew me up,
they raised me right.
And taught me at the end of the day,
I do not want to leave behind
an unfinished life.

Kindness is a Virtue

The more I grow up,
the more I realize,
stubbornness, ignorance, and impatience,
are not traits but a choice.
And there are people who choose those things
every. single. day.

Age

I wonder if once we grow old, will we count our days by
the could-haves and have-nots. Will the sun only kiss
our skin as autumn melts to winter frost? And then,
without much warning, suddenly our days are lost.
Left us to reminisce our times of glory within the
memories we forgot. I wonder if life will sit down with
me and have a coffee, like it's the first time we have
met. I wonder if age will say it's sorry, that time has not
forgiven us yet. I pause and think about those moments,
separated by the years. And wonder if we got our chance
or if the heartache was too feared. But if I could look
back, perhaps when there are wrinkles among my face.
Would I find that I regretted, living with such haste?
So, maybe in 50 years, my clock will stop its tic
and I'll wonder with my last breath…
if there was something I had missed.

Perseverance

After all, what are weeds if not will?

My Grandfathers Secret

The closest thing I ever saw
to true emotion in my grandfather
was when he was laying flowers at his father's grave.
His silent reverence towards the unknown,
as he placed two fingers to his mouth,
let out a sigh,
and placed them back on the stone.
The wind whispered a gentle reminder then,
that even as we share in love
there are parts in us,
unknown.

Main Character

How human of us
to remain so blissfully unaware
of all the lives
going on around us.

Wrong Century

I'm scared to use big words, so I dumb myself down,
confined to the limited speech
my generation was raised around.
Truth is, I'm scared of what they'll think of me,
perhaps call me things like broken, bolden, or weird.
The person who carries a vocabulary
awfully large for others to hear.
Using a language that doesn't go with the time,
but one hundred years ago, I'd be assuredly fine.
So, I believe therein lies the real issue,
I was born far too late
with words that are far too minuscule.
Never truly depicting how I specifically feel,
in a world content to never speak what is real.

Early Grave

If I die before I love,
I will have an empty heart.
If I die before I live,
I will have an unfulfilled existence.
So, I mustn't die without having done either of those,
because it would be as if I had never drawn a breath.
I would be long gone before I was actually dead.

From: The Future

Time will pass and as it does
you will hardly notice.
For you spent your time in so much fear
of a life that begged for your focus.

I Plead the Fifth

Yes, I am at fault.
Sometimes I see the world with shrewd eyes,
I pick and poke at things that are unfair.
There are days when my glass is half empty,
not half full,
and I do not always give more than I take.
But after all, I am human,
I am bound to make mistakes.
Yet, this shouldn't discredit my place in the world,
though the internet demands it does.
I must be a faultless girl, filled with patience,
the person society has raised me to become.
A picture-perfect model citizen,
held with beauty and flowing with grace.
In its haste, the world commands
my bad days leave no trace.

Eaten Alive

Don't you ever look at life with all its possibilities and
become overwhelmed?
Like at any second it could swallow you up before
you've even begun to live.

Humanity

Vanity and pride share the same stride,
though walking hand in hand,
they do not help me understand.

Hatred and anger have never been strangers,
bleeding from my veins,
and yet their message stays the same.

Exhaustion and fatigue are somewhat new to me,
though no amount of sleep,
could keep me from their reach.

Sorrow and despair whisper through the air,
if sadness were a sin,
I would surely be condemned.

Happiness and peace are last but never least,
their warmth is what I find,
has kept my heart so kind.

Dawning

Of all the nights I have dreamt my life away,
forgotten was the existence I fell asleep to.
My reality suddenly stood before me,
dressed in fulfilled hopes but on a body
too sad to remember what it was here for.
It walked over to me then
and whispered in my ear,
something I had always known
and something I had always feared.
It told me I was good enough,
and I would make it out there all alone.
So, then in the morning I awoke,
to a life that was suddenly my own.

The Heart of an Overthinker

They tell me to get out of my head
but so much of my life happens there
before it even reaches my heart.
Before it ever unfolds into life.
You've got to envision the life you want
before it can even begin.
Right?

Mixed Words

I am trying to learn not to stutter.
To not mix words.
To say exactly what I mean.
At least then, people can't say
they misunderstood me.

Welcome Home

There is something to be said for the way
we broach hard topics with the ones we love.
Taking on the tone we would use with a baby,
like we are suddenly afraid they are too fragile
to hold the news we are about to give.
Too young to know heartbreak.
Too soft to be made hard
and not yet ready
to face the rough truths of the world.

Gossip

One must have a small mind
to allow whispered words
to grasp and hold the idea
of someone's whole being.

Perspective

Maybe somethings we can't get back,
like a broken friendship made of glass.
And perhaps if we tried to put it together again,
there would still be cracks.
Never allowing a clear enough view
or understanding of what it had lacked.

Withered

I think it's quite sad sometimes,
when we knowingly let certain things die.
A plant you've been growing for months,
that never does.
So, you slowly stop watering it,
until suddenly it's gone.
A car parked in the garage,
in need of certain parts,
but there are more important things,
so it sits there some more.
A missed call from a friend,
who's always up to chat,
but you push it to tomorrow
and never call them back.
I suppose sometimes it's easier,
to swallow the defeat
for the things that you let go of,
that will never be complete.

Un-Learning

My favorite part about seeing how to do things right,
is figuring out why I did them wrong.

I Am Ready

What is the deadline to be grown up?
Is there some test I have yet to pass?
The contract I signed with life
said that it would happen fast.

What more do I have to prove?
Is there some essay I must submit?
The world promised that my age
would not deem me as unfit.

How many years do I have left?
Until I get to make the choices?
It seems the ability to drink
is what gives adults their voices.

What message am I missing?
Is there some secret I have lost?
Society demands that I behave
and that everything has a cost.

Where is this adulthood?
What year will it finally come?
My mother tells me to be patient
that it takes longer for some.

How much more time must I wait?
What's the holdup on my title?
I earned my way and being an adult
is truly very vital.

What happened to growing up?
Where have all the years gone?
It seems that my childhood
left me quick as a yawn.

Fingerprints

My hands tell the story of my life.
Every scar, every crooked finger, every wrinkle.
They show how I have fought,
how I've won, and how I've lost.
They are the building blocks of my humanity
because everything I have touched
has left its mark on my hands,
while my hands leave their mark on the world.

These Are Just Words

You see, the issue with the alphabet
is that sometimes it fails me.
These letters, all 26 of them,
do not always feel adequate.
Like the words, I would want to use
in moments like this,
haven't been discovered yet.
So, I blaze a path across the paper
armed with nothing but a pen and ink,
hoping that what materializes
is everything I need it to be.
Though oftentimes, this is not the case
and I fall short in far more moments
then I show grace.
But then I'm reminded,
poetry is not something to be found
and I forget that words are pointless
because it's in actions where they're bound.

Piano Man

Happiness is not meant to be written about
Poetry is meant for the damned
The burdened, broken, and beaten
The lonely, heartbroken, and banned
I have no words of encouragement for the optimists
I do not plant seeds to be grown
But I can weave a fair chorus full of longing
For the ones who are needing a home

Life's Game

Convinced that I am an old soul
shoved inside the body of a person
who will never look their age
and living in an era
where I will always feel
out of place.

Dream

If you asked me how to spell 'dream'
I'd tell you it was a five-letter word,
in some cases, it's a verb,
and to me it sounds like-
"I'm proud of you" or "I love you".
It has two vowels in it
and if you say it correctly or slow enough
it can feel like comfort and sometimes like home.
It gives you a reason to wake up.

If you asked me how to spell 'dream'
I'd tell you it starts with a hope
and it ends with an 'm'.
Don't ask me to define it though,
it means something different to every person.
To some, it's what longing is made of
but to me, it's a desire slightly out of reach.

If you asked me how to spell 'dream'
I would give you an honest answer,
but mostly I would tell you to be careful.
Not to use it so often
and make sure you have time.
Because while the word does exist
in dictionaries and in heart,
a dream is just a thought
until you write it out and start.

Worry

Someone once told me not to worry about things
that have not happened yet.
After all, humans are a part of nature
and nature never worries how things might end.
But what if it does…
I think the birds worry about the winds from the North
and the ants worry about the rain when it storms.
I think the trees worry about space left to grow
and the flowers worry about their buds in the snow.
I think the rivers worry about a drought when it's hot
and the fish worry about their fins when they're caught.
I think humans worry a lot more than they say
but I think nature might confess,
it worries the same.

Read Between the Lines

The problem is
I'm bursting with so much life,
and love, and passion,
I don't know where to put it all
except within words.

I've Already Existed

I want my words to mean something
but a part of me is scared they already do.
To some old soul who sat down years ago
and decided to string the same letters together
as the ones I'm writing now.
I'm scared all my thoughts have been recorded
then stored somewhere to collect dust on a shelf.
That all my sentences have an expiration date
already past, and I'm just writing things down
that have already been mapped.

Ignorance is Bliss

I am kind in my arrogance of the world.
I am cruel in my knowledge of its people.
To be a good human,
I must remain blissfully unaware.
Otherwise, I forsake all those I am near.

Racing Thoughts

Bit by bit,
I am beginning to understand
that life has a mind of its own
and it's hard to build anything solid
on moving ground.

Two Lives

I feel cheated somehow,
like life robbed me of my free will
and tore up the contract I didn't know I signed.
There's no real comparison to how I ended up
and the person I wanted to become,
because she has never existed.

She has never walked in my shoes,
been slapped on the hand one too many times,
and grew up watching her world slowly die.
Still, I feel like this wasn't how it should have been,
it doesn't seem fair that I've had to live with others' sins
while they washed their hands clean and walked away.

Call me a warrior, sure, but what am I fighting for…
Whom have I lost to make life worth this battle?
Was it me?
Did I lose myself amongst the ruble and rust?
Between the boxes during moves or the misplaced trust.
Got a glimpse of good luck before I let it run out
because the world seems hell-bent on letting me drown.

So yes, I feel cheated because this wasn't my choice,
this wasn't my mess to clean without any voice
and I've heard all about the triumphs and wins
of people with far less than the life I was given.
But that doesn't take away the heartache and pain
from the girl I missed out on and the one I became.

Human Connection

You can save people just by talking to them.
You can kill people just by ignoring them.

Personal Concert

I don't write to sound pretty, intelligent, or nice.
I write because words form songs in my head
and as I mumble to myself,
they create symphonies in my mind.
Then I must write them all out
so, the tunes not confined.

MORE

I've been craving a little bit more lately.
A little more time.
A little more sleep.
A little more love.
I've been hollowing out this space inside of me,
trying to make room for it all.
Burdening myself with the crisis of living,
while missing out on so much life.
Because this idea of 'more' seems so attainable
until I get ready for bed at night.
Close my eyes,
drift off to sleep,
in the same amount of time,
that I will always keep.
So, then it seems 'more'
can only be achieved in dreams.

Sleepless Thoughts

What use is a body well-rested
if the mind never shuts off?

I Don't Want Fairytales

My teenage years were filled with fantastic stories
of witches, wizards, vampires, and werewolves.
Sometimes even the occasional fairy tale.
Until as far back as I can remember,
I so longed to be one of those characters.
To be enveloped in a love story
so deep it spanned centuries.
To be included in a tale as old as time.
To contribute towards something beyond ordinary life.
I'm not sure exactly when the shift happened
but those dreams of being something so transcendent
came to an eye-opening stop once I realized,
the stories never chose the girl who remained
independent.

Seasonal Depression

I can hear the birds chirping again.
Maybe this is what it feels like to be at peace.
Finally, being able to listen to them sing.

Mature

They asked me to be strong
but didn't tell me why.
Told me I'd be wise
if I didn't bat an eye.
Witnessed many things
with this careful little gaze.
Listened to the whispers
adults would never say.
Questioned every action
but believed in all the words.
Marked my heart off limits
because love just seemed to hurt.
But through it all I couldn't tell you
the moment that I lost,
this tiny little piece of me
that some call childhood.

Freedom

And then it finally stuck.
I could do and be whomever I pleased.
So long as it only hurt me.

Don't Be Fooled

I can't remember exactly what age I was,
but one day I put away my toys for the last time.
Stopped reading fairy tales and fantasy.
Closed my dress-up drawer with all the glittery shoes.
Packed up everything used to label me as a child.
And stepped into a version of myself
I thought the world expected.
An adult.

Moving Forward

I try to forgive and forget
so, I don't live to regret.

The Art of Every Day

I feel like I'm slowly dying
from this subtle art of mediocracy.
Bending and shaping life
into this terrifying beautiful disaster.

Desire

I wanted you so bad until I had you
and then you weren't enough.
Sometimes, I'm the bad guy too.
I wish I was sorry.

Pulling Weeds

I figured if I stopped pouring water on things
not meant to grow,
I might finally see the sun again.

Keeping to Myself

Slowly figuring out where I belong in the world
Taking baby steps at falling in love
Starting at a crawl towards my future
Tiptoeing through the late nights
Whispering to all my accomplishments
Not everything has to be done so big and bright
It is often things that are the slowest
The most silent, which mean the most
They make the strongest impact and the greatest boast

Medusa

The anguish I feel so deep in my bones
has ruined my outlook,
turned me to stone.

TAG

I don't chase.
If I wanted to play tag,
I would go back to elementary school
where you could tell me you liked me on the playground
and I could pretend not to hear you.

There is not enough time in a day
to sit on a merry-go-round,
hoping you'll make it to some other destination
and not just the same circle.

I'm not perfect.
I'm not above the adrenaline rush
or the butterflies that accompany
trying to catch something just out of reach.

But I won't run after it with all my speed,
as my feet fumble beneath me
and I can hear the other children laughing,
when I trip and bruise my knees.

We're not kids anymore and now when I go home
where my mom can help bandage up my scraps.
She does not laugh quietly to herself
like she did when I was young
and thought love was a new thing.

Instead, she shakes her head,
tells me to be careful.
To watch where I'm walking.
That she doesn't want to lose me, not again.

So, please forgive me for not playing this game.
There is no winner in this thing called love.
And I don't chase,
not after you and not anymore.

Under Construction

I romanticize the curves of you
the roundness of your heart,
how you move with so much fluidity
it's a wonder you don't fall apart.
I romanticize the soft edges to you
because mine are so ragged and rough.
My heart is like a brick
and you never wanted anything that tough.

The Fine Line

There are days when sometimes
even I cannot find the line
between what is right
and what is real.

Overachiever

I have always been early at things,
early to rise,
early to walk and talk,
early to read and write,
early to sleep,
early to love,
but especially early to leave.

Dreamer

What if I choose wrong?
Why doesn't anyone ever talk about that possibility?
Sure, the grass may be greener on the other side
but what if the sky turns white,
and the sun is nowhere to be found.
Like it's been tucked away behind the earth,
left to drown…
Maybe I accomplish all of my dreams
without ever examining the cost
and then once I have everything I want,
it's still not enough.
Perhaps I can finally buy a home
somewhere peaceful and quiet,
just to discover there's no closure to be found
when it's suddenly too silent.
What if I choose wrong?
Pick someone else.
Move too far.
Skip the perfect song.
What if the consequences of a racing mind
and an overwhelmed heart,
mean I'm always on the cusp of lives
where I can never take part.

Hurting

The Fates are Doomed

If ever there were two souls destined to meet,
I would beg fate to let us be.

All the Red Flags

I should come with a warning sign
"Stay away. Don't waste your time."
I am a barren ground,
a place for haunted souls to be found
but not linger too long
or my mind will kick them out.
Devoid of certain emotions,
they don't present themselves anymore,
but I can promise you a good time
during the short span you're here for.
Because I'm a happy kind of person
with a positive and simple outlook.
Letting light and love pass through me
though, the latter leaves me shook.
Yet, most of the time I can't catch up
to this person whom I claim.
She floats along beside me,
calling out my name.
Attendance drills are mandatory
for the ones who enter my life
and tardiness or absentees
are only tolerated twice.
Though I never take it personally
when your time to leave has come,
you'll be just another checkmark
by a name that leaves me numb.
And after that, you can forget me,
while I try to do the same.
My warning sign should be labeled,
"Caution, her heart cannot be claimed."

Can't Wake Up

I feel like I'm chasing after broken dreams
trying to manifest themselves into nightmares.

Contradictions

Most people write about being hurricanes or storms, always mentioning the destruction they leave, like it's some kind of norm. No one ever writes about the black hole. A lonely darkness frozen in time. Somehow always on the outskirts of life. No one ever writes about the calmness that occupies sadness or anger. The destructive power of isolation, leaving those you love feeling like strangers. I wish someone would write about how it feels to hold emptiness, dark and seething. Like at any moment an unwanted guest could quietly sneak in. But I suppose I understand, the intrigue isn't there. Black holes are not reckless compared to what hurricanes would dare. They are loud and foreboding. No one questions their existence. Every coast knows the name of at least one worth a mention. So, perhaps it's with reason that no one writes about space because to describe its existence would put hurricanes to shame.

The Silent Enemy

I stare at the words I write and try to find fault in them
Like my pen could be lying
My paper could be scheming against me
I don't know how I got to this place
A place where I don't even trust words written in ink

A lesson in detachment:

It creeps up on you,
slowly and then all at once.
It appears as a ghost,
one you'll feel but never see.
Reaching out and holding you close,
refusing to let you free.
It lets you believe you've felt something,
a shimmer or a spark.
Then just like that it takes it back,
placing you in the dark.
Confined to a prison all your own,
a sanctuary in your mind.
Detachment is the game,
you end up losing to
with time.

A Million and One Galaxies

Maybe I am like a shooting star,
only destined to be seen in one galaxy.
Forever passing by a steady sun,
or the people I love,
who only seem to see me for a second
and then I'm off,
back to dust.
Blazing a path that onlookers can view
but no one could ever touch.

Coincidence

Maybe it wasn't love.
Perhaps those weren't butterflies in my chest
but ants running from a flood,
trying to build a shelter to get out of the mud.
And maybe the reason my hands shook in yours
wasn't because of nerves,
but because earthquakes were rattling under my skin,
trying to stop something before it begins.
It's possible the days that we talked,
weren't brighter because you were in them,
but because a sunny day was what
the weatherman had predicted.
Maybe it wasn't love.
I could chalk it all up to adrenaline,
the weather, and a tiny disaster.
But what if for a moment it was,
and life gave me all the signs that poets dream of.
How tragic would it be if I missed my one shot,
at a coincidental love,
that I never gave thought.

I Didn't Know the Rules

You were always you.
I was only practice.

I was always me.
But you were only practicing.

Corporate America

I'm unhappy,
Not the kind of unhappy that you feel one day,
and wash off the next.
Boiling water would not be able
to get this fatigue off my skin.
The world revolves around me on repeat.
Wake up. Work. Eat. Do it again.
My soul frowns at my computer screen
as my heart turns to dust.
The sun seeps through my windowpanes,
but can humans even rust?
Because it feels like my joints are mended together,
my hands ready to crumble off.
The keyboard sends no thanks,
even after I power it off.
My mind is set on rewind.
Did I eat? Did I move? Have I showered?
Another meaningless day that flew by in an hour.
An endless to-do list that keeps adding up.
A new notification on my watch
telling me to stand up.
But I can't stand, I can't sit,
I can't even think for a second,
because if I do, I don't allow myself
to be in the present.
In all the moments I've been through
and all the moments I've lost.
This life seems so worth living
but sometimes it's not.

A Conflicted Existence

My body is trying to convince me that I'm alive.
My heart is trying to show me how to live.
My mind is trying to tell me that I'm not worthy of it.

BUT

A simple three-letter word,
one that seems to always show up in my life
and not in the ways I want it to, like:
"…but wait, there's more"
"…but that was amazing"
or even,
"…but I love you"
No,
instead, I'm stuck with:
"I want you but…"
"you're great but…"
and even,
"I love you but…"
Isn't it a crazy difference,
the placement of three letters can make?

A Million Lives. A Million Loves

But I wasn't the love of your life too?
You have consumed mine.
Maybe you have lived too many lives
to remember which one I belong to.

The Past that Haunts me

I’m sorry.
Let me apologize now before you take my hand.
Not for anything I have done
but for everything I have yet to do.
The mistakes I have yet to make.
The decisions I have yet to change.
I’m sorry.
That I can’t talk to you about certain things,
ones that hurt me in my past.
I’m scared if I speak them to you,
let you hold them and tell you who I am.
You will be able to use them
and hurt me, once again.

Hollow

I want to breathe in and feel no hurt.
I want my lungs to work the way they used to,
before I met you and you took my breath away
but forgot to give it back.

I want to taste oxygen once more.
Feel it on my lips as I breathe in
like how it felt when you kissed me before a fight,
before you fled, leaving me breathless once again.

I want to feel the rush of euphoria.
Like when you used to stand near me,
just so my body can pump blood normally
and not leave me deprived of a basic human need.

I want to scream at you, tell you to come back.
That somehow, we'll make it right
but words feel like needles in my mouth
and when I try to speak, no words come out.

Because you left me.
You walked straight out the door
and now these three little words
have never made my lungs feel as hollow

…. as they do right now.

I Choose Life

I get rid of flowers before they are actually dead.
I call it "Fall" before the seasons ever change.
I switch the song before it has time to end.
I let go before the other person does.
I say goodnight before it's dark
and goodbye before it's time.
Mostly because,
I cannot stand to watch things die.

Pressing Pause

I don't think there is ever a proper time to say goodbye.
It happens in the midst of living.
It begins in one time frame and then
abruptly ends.

What If…

What if we never get it right?
And I can hear fate laughing,
saying it was always our time.

What if I end up with someone else?
And you place a ring on a finger,
that isn't mine.

What if all our plans go unfinished?
And I move away from this place,
our memories on rewind.

What if I only think of you on good days?
And the weather's only warm
because your light shined.

What if I start to forget you?
And then suddenly you're a jailor,
judging my crime.

What if I spend the rest of my life searching?
And the only thing I can grasp,
is what we left behind.

What if love could have saved us?
And we proved that destiny,
could not be designed.

What if I never get over you?
And then I use that like a shield,
take it as a sign.

What if you were my person?
And these what-ifs run around,
forever in my mind.

Sadness

My grandmother looks at me
and wonders why I am so deep.
I look in the mirror
and simply want to weep.

Insecurity

Tell them I was the sun reincarnated.
That I shone brightly through your room,
even on dark days.
Tell them that I was never battered or bruised,
not until what you did to me,
knowing what you knew.
Tell them I was the definition of kindness,
until I let you walk all over me,
like a doormat in the rain.
Tell them whatever you'd like about me,
but tell them the truth.
That I never lied,
never judged,
never used what you told me against you.
Make sure you mention every fight,
every accusation,
every invisible punch thrown.
Include all the blocked calls,
foul language,
and the way you let my image drown.
Tell them I was everything you said you wanted,
but continually pushed me away.
And that you couldn't tear me down enough
to make me need to stay.

Shipwreck

I harbor a love for you that I do not understand.
It is fleeting and fast-moving all at once.
Some days it is like a cat and only comes out,
only shows itself when everyone is gone.
When the peace and quiet become too loud,
your love comes to do some shattering.

Other days it is like a leaf falling from a tree.
Slowly ebbing and flowing into a space in my heart.
A place on the pavement I didn't know existed.
Landing lightly and with poise,
convincing me that trees do not make noise.
And surprisingly I stumble over this soft leaf,
this soft love, every time.

Then there are days my love rages like a storm.
Waves hitting the shore, too hard.
The currents rolling, too fast.
On these days, my anger resurfaces
like a ship floating back from a wreck.
The sailors must piece back together
all the places they didn't inspect.

Still, the winds keep on blowing.
They do not give a damn
about the consequences of loving someone
or the damage you command.
And these days get jumbled together,
a jigsaw in my mind.

My love for you runs rampant
and you don't bat an eye.

2am

Broken thoughts leave me like
the pieces of you that I left behind
and the lies I tell myself at night.

Throw Away the Key

Secrets come to die in me,
they go no further than a brick wall.
I'm a safe landing spot for most,
a permanent "welcome" mat on the floor.
Easy to move about and easy to talk to,
but hardly ever opening up
and never letting anything out.
It's a good place for secrets,
a quiet dumping ground for lost souls,
to be heard and understood.
and sometimes found.
Secrets come to die in me,
not because I let them
but because I never make a sound.

Relationship Illusions

I've lost you where I found you.
Not entirely whole but not completely broken.
Sad to mistake the two.
Even when it was right there in plain sight.
Didn't reach far enough to get it.

Solitude

I have no one to stand by me at my wedding.
No one to catch the bouquet once it’s thrown.
No attendees to attend a day about me
so, this life I will cherish alone.

Gut Feeling

I just know.
I would rather say that to let you go
instead of coming up with reasons I don't mean.
Ones like, "It's not you, it's me".

But technically that's true.
You wanted the life you had with me
more than the future
I saw with you.

I can't say things like,
"You didn't communicate enough"
because you did.
There was never anything that you hid.

I can't say it's because my family didn't like you,
or that you were mean in some ways.
We both know that's not true
because you always gave me praise.

To be honest, I don't know what to tell you,
there was no concrete thing you'd done.
For my heart to quietly tell me
my end with you had come.

There are no reasons I could give you
to lessen all the pain.
Just know the way you valued me,
I cared for you the same.

But this is where our story stops,
there are no excuses on my tongue.
Other than the fact that I just know
you're not my one.

Intoxicating

I'm starting to think that I'm an addict.
Addicted to all things "pretty".
Pretty faces.
Pretty lies.
Pretty distractions.
Obsessed with trying to find myself
in things that demand I be lost.
Searching for something to numb the pain
and dull the ache
of all the things the world wants me to be
and all the things I am not.
I'm an addict.
Scared to trust myself
without these so-called drugs.
Terrified the world has become empty
and without love.

Seeing Things

I want to be like a ghost.
To be seen and heard,
but never felt.
I want you to know
what it was like for me
when you disappeared.

Prisoner of War

All these years I've been raised up
and taught what's right from wrong,
handed down a suit of armor
and wrote on it, be strong.

As if the world needed a warrior
to fight for her and bleed,
another soldier among the ranks
begging to be freed.

A life spent in service of threats
that hadn't even come,
leaving me to wonder
why this mission felt so numb.

But in time I would learn
I was not meant to be in war,
hardened with the truth
that I was thoughtful to the core.

Battle-worn and quite exhausted
from a life spent on defense,
this tragic person in the mirror
made so very little sense.

Though the world's cruel
and its people have much to learn,
I wish the shield that I'd been given
had not been so stern.

So, while I'm proud of all the ways
you kept your head above water,
in the end the truth is that
I never wanted to be stronger.

Call Me

To the man who left my home but not my heart.
The one who wrapped me in praise
but never in his arms.
To the man who says he loves me,
the first man I made memories with.
The one who cared,
who comforted,
who wept with me.
Who held me up on his shoulders,
high above the world,
keeping me out of reach from harm.
To the man who let me fall
each and every day,
waiting for a simple gesture.
For a call.
The man whose name is rarely mentioned in my house.
The man whom I can no longer remember.
I do not smile at his face,
I frown.
He does not care what I am doing,
he's moved on.
From a little girl in pigtails
to a stubborn intelligent woman,
I need him no more.
To the man who was supposed to be my keeper,
I wish you were.

The Longest Mile

Do you know what I've learned?
Distance is distance.
It doesn't matter if you're 20 miles away or 2,000.
You're either with them or away from them
and it all hurts the same.

Thanks For Asking

I'm sick of people telling me I look tired. I know I do. The bags under my eyes are heavier than the weight of my sleepless nights. I say I'm fine like a bird would chirp from the cage it was born in. Content for a time. Most days I look in the mirror and don't even register what I see. A sullen ghost of the person that I used to be. It's not that I'm sad, though I'm definitely not happy, but try explaining that to my family. On the outside everything is fine because I've got a job, school, and time. So much time to do nothing but think, and dream, and ponder the places I'll never be. Of lives I've probably already lost and people I'll never meet. I am a prisoner trapped inside the body of a careless teen. But how am I supposed to care? Do it too deeply and I'm insane but care too little and suddenly I'm built of glass. Touch me and I'll crack. At least that's what I think people see when they look at me. But perhaps they see stone. Fall too hard and I'll shred you to bone. It's not that I'm lazy. I'm defeated. I'm young and old. Loving and cold. A walking contradiction if I've ever met one. I'm not sure how to hold onto something for longer than a moment when life slips past me, faster than the world I was born in. Everyone is moving too quick and I'm so tired of running a race I didn't sign up for. They say to just put one foot in front of the other. So, I walk straight into smothering puddles. My lungs close quickly and panic grips me like the cold death of night. I awake with a start and turn on the light.
Yes, I am tired.
Yes, I'm alright.

Self Less

I only know how to be wanted
when someone needs something.

To Be Young

I wish I could say I was fragile,
that the years have treated me well.
But I've got coarsened hands from wear and tear,
even my bones have begun to bend.

There's a thickness that surrounds my heart,
it has been there for quite some time.
And though many years have passed,
they all still live behind my eyes.

I wish I could say I was fragile,
though that would not be the truth.
My skin tells different stories
behind all this so-called youth.

Swimming Lessons

My bad days keep trying to convince me
that I'm drowning,
in a sea of all the things I'm not.
In an ocean full of relinquished hopes.
Treading water gets tiresome on these days
and I've forgotten how to float.

Life On The Line

What most people don't realize, is that I push myself to the edge for a reason. The edge of love and heartbreak. The edge of success and failure. I am almost always balancing on a line between self-improvement and self-disaster. But it's the only way I really know how to survive. This coping mechanism, I've learned, is what keeps me alive. It's either I feel everything so deeply to the point that I break, or I feel nothing at all and this life I forsake.

Enough

He's kind, enough.
He holds the door open for me,
but I walk on the outside of the street.
He's funny, enough.
He makes me laugh like no other,
but then ignores me for a day.
He's honest, enough.
He looks me in the eyes when talking,
but turns away when texting.
He treats me well, enough.
He doesn't say I'm beautiful or intelligent,
but he's sincere enough…
maybe he thinks it.
He doesn't hold my hand in public or hug me tight,
but he's caring enough so,
maybe he will one day just not tonight.
My mom says he seems like a nice guy.
My friend says it's time I found someone like him
so, that makes him good enough, right?
To settle down and build a home,
fill it with little feet running around.
Hope he has enough time to sit down for dinner,
ask me about my day.
Because even though it might not be
an all-encompassing love,
a love that 8-year-old me dreamed of,
a love that never leaves me with any "buts"-
It's enough just to be loved at all,
right?

Repeating Cycles

In this generation, the art of "the next best thing"
is slowly turning into, the art of everyday life.

The Cost of Being Human

The hardest moments come
when I can't feel a thing.
When the world stops at my feet.
When the rain pours
and the sea seems to swallow me whole.
Time slips by quickly here,
it is not bound by anything.
And these feelings, they wash over me,
but I'm stuck under the wave.
All my memories chase after me,
just hoping that I'll see.
In these moments I feel human,
but so much less like me.

Repentance

My sins come in the form of things I don't say,
messages I don't mean,
or responses I've delayed.
Sometimes I think about how beautiful it would be,
to speak everything I feel,
exactly when seen.

Loneliness

How sad the world can be
when one believes
and the other
does not.

Control

I woke up today.
I woke up angry, sad, and scared
but I woke up all the same.
So, one can only assume
that what I've been put on Earth to do
has not been accomplished yet.
And while that should ease a bit of fear,
perhaps grant a bit of grace,
for some reason I still worry
about the things I cannot change.

A Writers History

I have always lived my life by words.
Words that have meant something
and words that have hurt.

Mourning

A lesson in mourning:
it all feels the same.
Whether it's a beloved animal,
an appreciated friend,
or a quiet relationship.
A loss at the end of the day
is. still. a. loss.
No matter how insignificant,
a part of you leaves with them
and you'll never be that person again.
A small crack can still break.
So, mourn and be unashamed.
We all go through it,
just most in our own way.

Lost and Found

I waited for you to come back and tell me there was no one else like me out in that treacherous world. That you looked under rocks, across oceans, and in tiny towns for a single soul that could best my match. That you looked for a person to make you seem whole but found only half-filled souls. I waited for you to come back and tell me that the years you'd been gone, were simply spent playing hide and seek with the wrong sort of people. That at night when you craved warmth, you were only met with icy hands. A cold grip around your heart, making you miss my sunshine touch. I waited until I could wait no more. So, I went in search of you. Only to find breadcrumbs of the person you'd become. I found that after all this time of looking for you in crowded rooms, hoping you were just lost, and a long plane ride would be enough to bring you home.

You had found me in someone.

Flowers Don't Weep

If roses were like teardrops,
could we keep them in a bottle?
Store them tightly to mask the pain?
With the hope that water,
unlike petals,
would not wilt with age.

Friends

No, we can't be friends
because the truth is, we never were.
There was always deeper meaning to things you said
and hidden longing behind your words.
Though I cannot fault you for your desire,
perhaps I was your personal drug.
But a lonesome heart seems my curse in life,
even with your careful love.
I know you question if I felt the same,
did I ever wish for more?
In truth, what we had was terrifying
but you were whom I adored.
And maybe one day I will regret my actions,
I will ache to make amends.
But for now, you have to understand,
we cannot be friends.

The Giver

I have a bad habit of taking on other people's dreams.
I hear them talk about things with so much passion
that I want to love them too.
Even if it's something I couldn't fathom for myself.
I fall in love with their words.
I fall in love with their hopes.
I fall in love with them.
And eventually, I fall out of love with myself.
I don't know how to love without giving up all of me.
Even my own dreams.

Play Again?

After all I did for you.
After all you put me through.
Now I'm the bad guy?

Fair enough.
I suppose,
two is a better game.

Time Travel

I have never really asked for more time before,
have always accepted goodbyes for what they were.
A means to a lesson.
An end to a beginning.
Emotions that keep changing
the longer that you're living.
But just this once, I wish that time would lend me grace,
give me just a few more seconds before you slip away.
Hand me the minutes needed to make you mine again,
before I begin the days full of heartache that tie me in.
Make the hands on the clock finally stop spinning
so, we can have more time
and maybe start from the beginning.

The Absence of Nothing is Still Something

I have stayed silent during important talks.
I have hurt people and never apologized.
I have remembered people and never reached out.
I have left rooms when I was needed to stay.
Almost the same way that,
I have loved you as you walked away.

No

You told me that you loved me on a Tuesday,
only I wasn't quite prepared,
I thought we needed more songs to sing to
or more memories to share.
My mom told me she was married just after a month
and my best friend shared that she's only loved once.
I figured we would fall somewhere in between
the "I love you" and the part where you get on one knee.
Yet, here I now stand with a decision to make,
a one-word answer with a whole life at stake.
The movies always say this moment is bliss
but my heart is in turmoil, and I only feel sick.
Because I'm not sure I can give you all that you want,
a ring on a finger is something I never gave thought.
So, you silently watch as I blow out our flame
and sadly I know I'll never see Tuesdays the same.

Dawns

There is a pot cracked down the middle
at your parents' home,
the result of an over ambitious game of war.
There is a T-shirt in my dresser I can't quit wearing,
an inside joke to mark where you're from.
There's a broken bit of fence by the corner of the house,
but if you ask, no one has noticed it yet.
There are songs on a playlist I no longer listen to,
too close to the memories I can't quite forget.

Healing

Irony

I do not write love poems,
they evade my space.
Allowing me only small glimpses
into what it takes
to create something so beautiful
and still so full of grace.

Onto the Next

If I'm being honest…
there are certain songs I can't listen to anymore,
ones that are permanently on skip.
There are places I can't go to anymore,
forever taking the long way home.
Certain things I can't eat and certain people I can't meet.
It's not because I still love you,
but because I will never forget the love I had for you.
A part of you that will always be a part of me
and certain things like that,
I just don't care to repeat.

Nostalgia

I do not trust nostalgia.
She is grief in the hands of happiness.
Full of cumbersome memories,
ones that aren't quite welcome.
Yet, they are still so full of hope and longing,
for something that was…
or never got the chance to be.

She slips through the door on a chilly day,
then lights a fire and sits down,
taking advantage of my warmth.
She tries to convince me it's always been this way,
Warm, and cozy, and happy.
That sadness and anger have never existed.

But I know better.
Because the fire reminds me,
while it is lovely to look at and pleasant to sit by
it burns when you get too close.
It was not created to hold
and just like nostalgia,
she only comes on the days it is cold.

This is Not Therapy

There was a moment where I realized
I needed to stop punishing my body
for how my mind was feeling.

I Am Still Learning

I went to share a writing today,
the only request was that it be happy.
Happy….
I searched for the word in my poems,
tried to find the theme of it woven into words,
looked for the feeling even amongst a single verse.
What I discovered is that I am not a happy person,
I'm a hopeful person still healing wounds I don't air.
I learned that my words were never meant to be shared
and they are filled with things I never found peace in,
but most of them, give my writing some reason.
The majority of my thoughts are bitter and cold
but they leave room for light,
they leave room for hope, and love, and time.
And perhaps I am not happy
but that doesn't mean I will never know its meaning.
Maybe I'm making room
by leaving my closet door open,
finally facing the place where my monsters are sleeping.
Maybe I cannot write about the happy moments
because they are the only piece of me, I get to keep.
And my words are just the consequences
within the writings that I reap.

Past Me

Most days I do not feel seen,
only a projection of the person
that people want me to be.
I wonder how many versions of myself
are out there sitting idle,
frozen in time.
A curated person
who is no longer mine.

Stolen Time

I'm a serial procrastinator,
always waiting until the last second.
To finish work.
To book the trip.
To say what I feel.
To let go…
A part of me believes that the longer I hold out,
the faster it will take to see it through.
The quicker I'll be able to be done.

Timing

I wasn't ready,
and I hate to say that's the truth.
That the reason I missed out on us,
missed out on you,
was because I couldn't figure out how to be loved.
How to open my heart up big enough
to allow a four-letter word into a burdened soul.
I couldn't wrap my head around the thought
that I wasn't flawed in some shape or form,
or that you wanted me regardless of what I offered up.
Because in truth I still don't know what I would do
if you were to reach back out and hold me close,
not pull away when I asked you to go.
I'd like to think that time has healed me just a little,
enough to accept the affection
and make whatever we had feel official.
But what I know now is sometimes
timing is off for a reason,
because you wanted me when I wasn't quite ready
and yet, here I am now
with a heart that is steady.

Short-Term Memory Loss

I get stuck on you
like an unfinished thought.
One second,
it's there
and then,
it's not.

Roses Are Overrated

I once dated a boy
who seemed simple and kind,
but much like thorns on a rose
looks never bite.
I spent years figuring out
how to hold onto that love,
pricked by the thorns and putting it off.
I had this idea
that the thorns could be changed,
and a love like we had
could somehow be tamed.
After years spent together
it finally clicked,
no matter how you hold a thorn,
you still end up pricked.

Your Lesson to Me

You were everything I needed to learn
and nothing I needed to keep.

The Strongest Organ in the Human Body

Hearts cannot be broken.
They can be battered, bruised,
and bent to be unrecognizable
but they cannot be shattered
into all unknown pieces.
Because even after a devastating fall,
a splintering moment,
a shuddering stop.
Your heart, one that's felt so much pain
and so much loss,
is the only thing that keeps on beating
even when everything else stops.

Some People Still Don't Learn

I've always thought it was kind of ironic
that in order to see if something was hot
you had to sip it first
and wait to see if it burns.

Star Crossed

People keep telling me the things meant for my life
will not pass me by.
In a way, this makes sense
and brings me comfort somehow
because you had always seemed like a shooting star.
Blazing a beautifully bright path across the night,
making me reach out my hand and touch the sky.
Only to be burned time and time again,
trying to catch a flame that kept on moving.
It made me wonder why I was never enough.
How something as brilliant as what we had,
could end up being so rough.
And then one night, I understood at last.
You cannot force things to stay,
if they're only meant to cross paths.

Closure

I drive to all our old spots,
even though you are no longer with.
You are no longer there.
I was hoping to get a glance at you,
us,
the way we used to be.

I drive to all our old spots,
only they are not ours anymore.
They are up for grabs now,
willing to be given to someone new.
Willing to be everything we're not.

I drive to all our old spots.
This will be the last time.
This is my new start.

Coffee Shops

Hi…
I figure I should start off with that, instead of:
It's been a while since I've heard you laugh,
and I really miss holding your hand,
and the world has been so dull since you left,
that I forget to breathe every now and again.

What a small world!
I should probably say it's nice to see you
but I've never been a good liar
and to be honest, I hate you, or I used to,
or I thought I did once upon a time.
But when I look in your eyes, I just see us,
and it shouldn't make me smile but it does…

I hope you're well.
This is the truth because I honestly do,
I hope your life has grown all of the things
that even I couldn't give you.
I hope everything you were missing
is much better than all the things I lost
because this life seems so short, until it's not.

I've got to run.
Maybe we could grab coffee sometime?
I know we won't but that's the polite thing to say
and I know you don't mean your "sure"
as you walk away.
But deep down inside, my heart skips a beat
because now I'm hoping for the day that we'll meet.

Goodbye.
I think I mean it this time.
There was never anything good about crying
but I haven't done that in a while
and I'm sure it's because I'm forgetting your hugs,
or how I loved your embrace.
But time does a funny thing
by making everything okay.

Priorities

I always wonder what would happen
if I chose what was in my heart
and not my mind.

When the Lights are Out

I'm not scared of the dark
but my mind plays tricks on me when the lights are out.
Suddenly, I believe in monsters
and the made-up stories I heard around the campfire.
My eyes think they see things that aren't there,
and my ears believe sounds to be something
other than what they are.
I'm not scared of the dark.
But when I can't see, it's hard to trust the things
that are actually around me.
My imagination grows out of control
to the point that it scares me
and sometimes this reminds me of you.

The Zoo

I'm like a caged animal,
stuck within four walls,
trapped behind a single door.
Not sure if it's meant to keep me in
or to keep others secure.

Intuition

You get to decide what you need.
No one else.

Wishful Thinking

And I release you,
with a heavy heart full of hope
for everything we had
and regret for what we never got.
Though our strings are frayed and brittle,
I have still tied them in knots
and while I know it's not right
for me to hold onto the past,
I look forward to knowing you
outside this house made of glass.
And I know that in some way
this is all my fault, like everything else,
but you let go too soon
and walked away too fast.
Still, I'm done placing blame
and I'm done pressing pause
because life continues moving
even when you're gone.
So, I'll let go now
because my hands are quite tired
from holding onto a version of us
that has never transpired.

A Writing for You

I do not speak in love poems.
I am not fluent in that form of adoration.
But I am sure that is what you meant
when you said, "Write about me."
Though, I do not write about the dead.

This is Moving On

I used to spend my days reading words
because they reminded me of you.
Now I spend my days writing words
to remind myself of all that you've done.

Personal Space

See, that's the danger of it all.
The longer I'm alone,
the easier it becomes to find comfort in the silence.
To fall in love with the unforced hands
of my own thoughts.
So, it is not others that you should be afraid of,
it is my ability to be perfectly content with being alone,
which you should fear.

The Name I Do Not Speak

Him.
A name that I can no longer feel in my bones,
one I'm not too sure I can even pronounce.
An object, an it.
A face on a body.
No longer a person I can hold my emotions in
or take shelter from the rain with.

Him.
An indirect statement to mean another place,
somewhere far away.
Because I am here
and that is way too far
for me to do anymore guessing.

Him.
Another bridge burned
with no trace of an ember
because there are so many flames.
A reason to push myself harder
but to duck from attachment
and meaning.

Him.
Just another reason to stand up.
A word that holds no relevance in my life.
Much like a petal on a rose,
beautiful at first but lonely alone
and still at the end of the day,
I decide roses just aren't for me.

Him.
The name I will no longer say.
So now it is no longer him,
just me.

No Trespassing

There are hard lines
everywhere you look in my life.
Boundaries that are set.
Sometimes in pencil,
other times in pen,
but almost always in Sharpie.
Smudge-free.
No blurred edges here.
Refusing to be overlooked.
No chance of them getting crossed.
Because I will not be made a fool,
for being soft.

Take a Breath

Sometimes I find myself waiting
for the world to give me a sign
that I'm going down the right path,
that I am where I'm supposed to be,
or that I should do a certain thing.
Forgetting that I do not need to ask
for permission to breathe.

Gardener

I tell my therapist about you
like a garden would speak of the breeze,
blowing softly amongst the many flowers
and rustling all the leaves.

You no longer resemble water
though your presence still flows steady,
I no longer drown when you surface
and the flood's no longer deadly.

The sun cannot overpower me
when your memory shines through,
my stems are stronger than the rays
and my flowers continue to bloom.

You're no longer detrimental
and your absence isn't missed,
because there is new life in my garden
even though you still exist.

Poisoned Ink

I used to think about you
but not anymore.
Not since I picked up this pen
and began to write down these words.

Mutual Understanding

I need someone who will love me on my bad days.
My moody, messy, miserable ones.
The days that crawl up my throat like a bad dream.
The ones that make me feel alone
but careful, don't touch me or I might break.
Comfort is not a home on these days.

I need someone who will hold me
when I refuse to be seen.
When the lights stay dark.
When my windows stay closed.
Even the sun refuses to come in the door.
My head is bowed with a heart that's scorned,
a kind embrace may help heal from this one.

I need someone to show me how to trust.
The world is cold and bitter
and I have kept my distance from it,
for far too long, far too much.
Grasp my hand and hold it tight.
I promise I will join you in time.

I need someone to love me when I can't love myself.
When life pulls on my desires,
my passions, and sometimes my health.
I need another hand and a little bit more warmth.
Someone to help rescue me
from this love that's all torn.

Reflection

You don't know me.
You know what I allow you to see,
or hear,
or read,
or touch,
… but you don't know me.

Body Count

I refuse to be the property of broken men.
Ones who lick their wounds with women.
The ones who call it love when it's lust.
I do not belong in some little boys' secrets.
Held hostage by this game called "pretend".
Truth and trust seem to be options here.
Though, not for me.
Not for us.
Women who are strong, intelligent, and bold.
We do not date men "just because".
Though our survival depends upon,
a number, by our name, on a list.
Taken advantage of because of our hearts
when our guts sing different songs.
Listen to it we must,
for it's what makes us strong.

Healing

I am only as kind as my unhealed wounds.

The Sun Comes After the Storm

Loving me is like loving the rain,
accepting that it comes and goes,
that it's not meant to be controlled.
So, when it pours,
with raindrops pounding,
the land never questions
why it is drowning.

Loving me is not like loving the sun.
I am not bright all the time.
Sometimes there are days
when I hardly even shine.
I am not big, bold, and bolstering
but beautiful, yes.

See, I will not burn you if you get too close.
No, you will freeze to death first.
And then you will know
what it's like to love a storm.

Musings of the Mind

Some days I wake up as poetry.
Some days I wake up as a muse.
But most days,
it's hard to distinguish between the two.

Under The Same Moon

I think at the end of the day,
you will always have me.
In one capacity or another,
more than a friend but less than a lover.
There aren't enough words in the dictionary
to describe how this makes me feel
so, I will put it this way…
The sun still chases after the moon
even on rainy days,
leaves still grow on trees
knowing they'll be gone by winter,
and muscles still heal
even after they've been injured.
Mornings return after long sleepless nights,
hours spent wondering if life's worth the fight.
So, though I won't be with you in every waking moment
and perhaps we'll only share the moon between oceans,
I'll take shelter in knowing there's a person out there
that held who I am without any fear.
And if in some life things end up different,
at least we both know what it was
and what it isn't.

Warmth

You made all the years I'd spent alone,
worth the heartache,
worth the cold.

Expired

Creativity has an expiration date,
but I learned that lesson a little too late.
Took a little too long to write down these words,
to sing you these songs.
Got a little too caught up
in wondering if you were the one.
And now I'm just here trying not to miss out,
on the ideas or feelings that sometimes sneak out.
From a place where I'd buried them a little too deep,
that was until you loved this side of me.
So, now my creativity is something like fate
and yet, somehow, I still miss my "use by" date.

Survival of the Fittest

I owe the world no justifications
for the ways in which I choose to survive it.

Silence

I am not always spoken and carefree.
Sometimes words struggle to fall out of me.
But these days do not leave me debilitated.
Though I am burdened, broken, and bruised.
In these tender times, I am softly shaken,
filled with certain memories and moments,
I would rather not awaken.

Society has gotten to me

There are days I wake up and do not feel beautiful
or even the slightest bit interesting.
My shadow follows me around on days like these.
My reflection does not smile back at me.

There are days I wake up and feel like art,
brimming with potential.
I give life to everything I touch on days like these.
I even tend to give myself away.

The Life of a Poet

My words scream at me.
Inside of me.
Threatening the life of me.
Begging to come about.
Only then do I hear them.
Only then do I let them out.

Degree

One of my main gripes with life
is that it demands I be single-dimensioned.
Giving all of my focus and all my attention
into a specific aspect of living.
Devote all of my time and all my intentions
into just one thing that makes me human.

One of my main gripes with life
is that it keeps on moving and keeps on spinning.
But then I have to stand here stationary
and watch as life passes through me.
So, I'm grasping at memories trying not to be foolish
because I put all of my moments into just one solution.

I Forgive You Well

I was always taught
to never say things I don't mean.
Similarly, you don't cut down a garden
when it's green.
Still, I wish I could tear you down
all the same.
I suppose sometimes forgiveness,
is lighter than grief.

A New Faith

I have never believed in angels
or in that beautiful place far above.
I believed in what I could see
like the dreariness of a life, thereof.

Now my beliefs have been put into question
though, I understand why you could not stay.
And I do not blame you for growing tired
and gaining wings to fly away.

Gift of the Present

It is not your responsibility
to carry the weight of the past
on your shoulders.
It happened, you survived,
now, remember to live.

Unfamiliar

I think in a twisted way
he was too safe for me.
My thorns had nothing to cling to,
my darkness was overcast with light.
There was no part of my sad soul
that recognized itself in him.
And that is half the battle of love,
isn't it?
To be welcomed home like a friend
and not a stranger.

Paying Attention

The world is kind to me, most days,
and not the kind you get
as an appreciation or thanks.
What I mean is,
my coffee stays hot longer than it should
and my sweater keeps me warm
when it's suddenly too cold.
The rain passes quickly
as I'm driving someplace,
almost as if it's keeping me safe.
There's a roof over my head
with somewhere to sleep
and somewhere to stay.
These are the things I forget about
from day to day.
Strangers hold the door for me
when my headphones are in
and part of me wishes
I'd tell them what that meant.
The sun shines in my window
just when I need it the most
and the waves hold steady
when I ride down the coast.
There's not much to complain about
and this I am certain,
because the world is kind to me
on the days I'm not looking.

Depth

I wish I could tell you what that meant.
I wish I could dig some up,
pull it from these words,
and give it to you as a gift.
Maybe then you would understand,
depth is not something you just have.
It's something you're taught,
it's in the things that you've lost,
and I cannot just hand it away.
I cannot just tell you the things
that I need you to say.
Depth is not easy.
Depth is not light.
It's the heaviest thing I've carried,
throughout my whole entire life.
It will follow you around
like a half scary ghost.
But really, depth's just a word
lost amongst most.

Hoping

HOPE

It's a funny thing, hope,
the way it comes knocking at your door.
An unexpected guest.
A quiet visitor.
You welcome it with warm arms,
as it wraps you in its embrace.
You tell it to stay awhile
because it helps you feel safe.
The stories it speaks of then,
ones of success,
ones of love.
It reminds you of all the good in the world
and all the great things you have done.
It never stays too long.
For it knows where it belongs.
But it will always find a home in you,
especially when you do not feel strong.

Too Quick

Frozen toes by the water's edge,
I held you close to me.
Summer's gone and winter's come
but still, you were the same.
Miles up a mountainside,
the sky stretched on forever.
I wish I could say the same for us,
but now we both know better.

Lanterns

I am out wading in water
Swimming with the stars
Breathing in too cold air
Trying to free my heart

I am out with curiosity in tow
Looking aimlessly for a sign
Hands in my back pockets
A restless calm to my mind

I am out dancing in darkness
Spinning without any help
As careless as a child
I am out finding myself

Sixth Sense

I thought of you
and for a second
I knew,
that you were
thinking
of me
too.

Home

I am a lonely wanderer,
a quiet observer of life, of love, of passion.
Quickly becoming wary of anything that stays too long,
so, I move onto new things.
Forever with the hope that what is coming,
is better than what is gone.
And that maybe, just maybe,
something permanent will take root in my heart.
Forcing me to stop and stay,
just for a little while more.

Just In Time

The sad part is, that I will let you down.
Once, more than once, a thousand times,
and I won't be able to say sorry
because I'm giving you fair warning.
But if you're one of those people
who wear sunglasses when it's dark
or headphones when it's quiet,
then you will fall into my jumbled world
without even blinking, warning signs and all.
And maybe that's just the person I need,
maybe then we can show each other
how to forgive ourselves first.

The View

I hope every sky girl
finds her sky guy,
her do-or-die guy.
The "maybe I might try"
give a little effort,
spend a little time,
getting in the water,
splashing the tides guy.
So, in their ignorance
they just might find,
a type of love
worth a picture
of the sky kind….

Love Talks

I'm not sure exactly
about everything I want.
My mind likes to play games
with my decisions and resolve.
But my heart… oh, my heart,
she holds steadfast.
Her decisions will not waiver
in breaking free of the past.
She and I are in agreement
with the things I would want.
A person who holds my future
in the presence of their heart.
Someone who makes Sunday mornings
a little less cold, a little less quiet.
Someone who knows just how I like my coffee
and then is brave enough to try it.
A person who can hold the deepest parts of me,
the ones not on display for the world to see.
A person who bumps my head and holds my hand,
a gentle reminder to show they understand.
Someone with endless reasons to walk out the door,
to flee at first sight.
But someone who continually stays in spite,
of all the secrets I've buried
and all the scars that haven't healed.
I need me a person who makes love seem real.

faith:

being a passenger in a car
flying on a plane
mailing a letter
riding a roller coaster
sipping a hot drink
walking around barefoot
falling for you

Understood

I think what I want most in this life is simplicity.
The simplicity of being known,
of being seen
of being told,
that I do not have to hide who I am
just for someone else to hold.

The Silent Observer

I'm in love with deliberate movement.
The work of sure strokes on a blank canvas,
or that of a meticulous routine to start the day.
Steady hands have a hold on my anxious heart.
Watching in awe at the calmness
that accompanies a quiet soul or a rested mind.
Intentional patterns which create a colorful life,
unlike the one I live in black and white.
My mind gravitates toward unwavering motion,
consciously aware that I am chasing after
the very thing I could never have.
A stable life.

Perception is Key

I've found that life
is only half as good as you allow it to be
and half as bad as you make it out to seem.

Flatline

Happiness,
I have concluded,
is not meant to be a straight path.
It is not a steady journey
down a one-lane road
without any gaps.
Happiness,
I have decided,
is similar to life with ups and downs.
So, I try to keep this optimism
on the days when I'm
closer to the ground.
Happiness,
I have discovered,
is much like the human heart.
Because in the end,
the only flat line we get
happens when
we're gone.

Theatrics

I am the maker of my destiny,
though my lips can still be swayed.
But under proper circumstance,
you are the master of my play.

Unconditionally

I used to be scared to say I love you.
This only came after I found out
how conditional love could be.
Three simple words
which haunted me in my sleep.
That followed me around
like the broken pieces of a person,
I thought I should be.
I used to be scared to say I love you
before I found out love was freeing.
Before I felt it in my bones.
Before I let it fill my heart.
Now I hold onto love like a band-aid,
ready and willing to give it to anyone I see.
It is no longer a weapon I wield in desperation,
nor is it the thing that falls at my feet.
Love is rejuvenating.
Love is you and me.

Flowering

For she danced with the lilies in the spring air
because they matched her beauty.
Even without a word said, she felt whole.
And as they opened their leaves to her,
she began to bloom.

Peace

For once, I will sit down and have coffee with myself,
hoping my mug will still be warm
like it hasn't been left out for a while.
I will pour the creamer slowly
like I don't have somewhere else to be.
I will mix my sugar until all the little grains
are fully dissolved
so, that when I get to the last few sips
they are not tainted, too sweet.
I will sit and breathe and relish in a moment
that is so often lost amidst a daily routine.
Like life is the thing moving around this moment,
not during it.
For once, I will drink my coffee presently
and I will ask myself
where I am at in life… I hope the response is,
"you are exactly where you need to be".

Blind Trust

Unguard your heart
Let it carelessly be mine
Just do it
Just this once
One more time

I promise I won't drop it
I'll pinky swear it
if I must…
Please trust and understand
I mean you no harm
No foul
No damage done

I see it quite simply
Your heart should be mine
That thing beating in your chest
Full of little butterflies
Just waiting to rest
And hoping to fly

I'm no enemy to you
I'm a friend, not a foe
You're the one I have searched for
Past, present
High and low

So let down your walls
Leave them unchained
Hand me your heart
and we'll be on our way.

The Traveling Homebody

There are days I would like to sing with the birds,
happy and carefree.
Then there are days that the trees reach out,
long limbs and roots deep.
There's a war between myself and I,
a balancing act,
a game of give and keep.
Do I join the birds and fly away?
Or do I let my feet take seed?

Puzzle Pieces

In this world, I'm not lost.
I'm just looking for all the little moments
that add up to being found.

Spontaneity

I get called impulsive,
spontaneous, and sporadic,
like it's a bad thing.
Like life is meant to be lived seamlessly,
no sudden adventure,
no need for change.
I get told I am supposed to fall aimlessly
into the mundane.
Question nothing,
and take it day by day.
As if there are no answers to be found,
like my soul could fit the mold
of this tiny town.
So, maybe I am reckless
and in the long run I'm losing.
But how freeing it seems,
to live a life of my choosing.

The Alphabet

Stringing together 26 letters of the alphabet
differently every day, can become heavy.
And there are even days when I must claim defeat.
Days where I place my pen down
as the words bring me to my knees.
But my body is always there forcing me to stand up.
To stand tall.
To be proud of all this deepness,
which I've carried in my heart.
Reminding me that these letters, all 26 of them,
are just an extension of that part.

Lust

To the next person who will get access to my skin,
you'll need to have forever
whispered among your fingertips.
Glide them over me in a purposeful caress, saying,
"you're safe, you're seen, and I will not let you forget".
My body will no longer be a vessel of choice,
whims of desire left brittle and coarse.
I am no longer fluent in the language of lust,
though love has time to still claim my trust.
And when it does, because it eventually will,
my arms will be waiting, and my heart will be still.
There will be no fear when I ask it to stay
and I will tell it the stories of times I had strayed.
Of nights spent lonely, though I wasn't alone,
and mornings in despair of warmth that felt wrong.
Because I'm more than a body and more than a face.
Worth more than a guilt trip or someone's "mistake".
So, any intimacy gained from earning my trust
is something the right person will not try to rush.

Do I go to church?

All this talk of mind, and heart, and soul.
Yet, still so little talk of what it means,
and why it happens,
or where it goes.

Senses

I see you in the snowflakes
that fall around my face
and in the sun that shines through my room.
I feel you when the wind
wraps me in an embrace
and when the flowers begin to bloom.
I hear you amongst the rain
as it taps along the ground
and sometimes as the birds sing their song.
I remember you when I smell
something sweet that I've found
and in moments that remind me to be strong.
I view the world differently
now that you have left
but your presence still has not yet gone.
These cherished little moments
feel more like a theft
without you here to help me up past dawn.
So, I'll go about daily life
in search of something past
with new distractions to help me push through.
But I won't forget
and I know this at last,
somewhere out there, you can see me too.

To Be Gentle

I like a soft love,
an unrushed warmth,
something that is tender and kind.
That sweeps light under closed doors
and invades the frigid parts of me,
turning them golden,
making them shine.
Leaving any vacancy full,
with every reservation blurred,
creating a morning that is much more,
mine.

Rodney Strong

I've never been a fan of wine before.
In fact, the Italian in me laughs at my unease
towards the red liquid that stains your lips pink.
But then on a random winter night,
following a short-winded flight,
I found out that wine wasn't just a drink, it was an art.
Because you picked out the bottle and spoke of the taste
you ended up showing me a bit of your heart.
You poured me a glass and told me to swirl my cup,
said it's what the pros do when trying not to act drunk.
Our conversations morphed into something quite deep,
the red liquid melting all the walls that you keep.
But to be honest, my drink didn't taste much like beauty,
it was just slightly too bitter but maybe I'm choosy.
So, if you were to ask me what I learned from that night,
I'd tell you how to fall in love,
over a single glass of wine.

On why I'm a romantic:

The most love I have ever given
was to a person who did not even
reciprocate the feelings.
So, I can only imagine
how in love I will be
when I find the person
who is actually meant for me.

Happy Balance

I choose to see all the good in life
and let the bad brush off.
So, I do not dwell on what
would rather keep me down.
I choose to remember all of the things
that remind me to be a better person.
Everything, I can no longer write about.

Life's Not Over

Often times, I start to think I am tired of life,
that my stay here on Earth has seen its brightest days.
When the stress of living becomes too burdensome
I start to count my days, one by one.
Understanding that sometimes what is left
is not always better than what is gone…
But then I come up for air when I am underwater
and close my eyes when the plane starts to land.
I stand for far too long enjoying a hot shower
and get excited when I find a new band.
I keep writing these words with hope that another,
will find the courage they need
to stay a day longer.

Equality

And then I realized that we were all the same.
Straining our necks, just to get a glimpse of the ocean.
Reaching our hands up, trying to touch the sky.

Life Sentence

The most impactful thing I've ever heard was when someone told me that we are simply tourists here on earth. We cannot stay forever. Our existence is merely but a fleck in time. No amount of love I give will change that course, nor love received change mine. So, I know one day that I will go, regardless of everything I tried, and death will come to claim a suitor without ever batting an eye. Though this idea should terrify me and perhaps I should crumble, sob, or weep. But the idea of non-permanence leaves me somehow feeling free. So, no matter what I choose in life, be it hatred, love, or grace, my time here on this planet is one that moves with too much haste. And perhaps this is all meaningless and we're just programmed or designed. Created just to take up space, to break and bleed with time. But still, I choose to look at the world with a different set of eyes. Because in the end, life is short, and I don't plan on wasting mine.

The Revolving Door

Can you live without me?
If your answer is yes, please leave.
Take all your attachments and promises with you,
my home has no room in it for half fulfilled truths.
Pack up all your boxes and crumpled messages,
dust the cobwebs from the corners of me,
all the forgotten pieces you couldn't see.
Take your clothes and your suitcase,
and the future I thought I wanted.
Pack it all up, nice and neat to tuck away,
into a drawer you'll never open again.
And go.
The door will close and then reopen for someone new.
Someone who won't want to do this thing called life,
without me.
I know it will.

The Perfect Orchestra

I keep going through my memories of you
like strings on a piano.
Muscle memory takes over
and I know exactly what to play.
Like second nature,
you were suddenly the missing piece
in my melody.

Earth

When you really think about it,
we live on a floating rock,
spinning around floating gas,
in a galaxy full of wandering dust.
With no real purpose.
No real mission.
No promise of tomorrow.
Why wouldn't you do the thing you want?

Prince Charming

I would like to apologize to younger me.
The one who climbed hills to feel strong,
spent half her life singing songs about love,
dreamt most of her nights about a guy
she'd call "the one".

I feel like I have let you down a little bit.
Tucked my heart away with yours on your sleeve
because the years have not been kind to me. To us.
I know you'd tell me; mom says that's not an excuse,
I know that you're right, and there's nothing I can do.

But my heart breaks a little bit more each day
for the girl who watched Cinderella like a religion,
the one who thought the hero always beat the villain.
I am sorry to say that I have not been faithful
I have strayed away from hope and grace.
Stopped believing in someone who'd sweep me away.

Though I'm still not quite sure what to explain
because did I give up on love or was it all just a dream?
One that an innocent child held with belief,
convinced there was a soul out there just like hers.
But that makes about 7 billion people to sort through,
far too many for my life to consume.

To have ask me about my day or my favorite color
even though I know that my world has grown duller,
when yours was always so vibrant and bright,
pages filled with little hearts, initials, and plus signs.
And oh, how I wish it was all still that easy,
the playground is where I'd find the man of my dreams.

So, I feel this is where I should place my apology,
I'm sorry to the girl who just wanted to love
because I haven't quite yet found a man that's enough.

We'll Meet Again

I do not look upon death
and demand a refund on the pain.
I look at death and tell it to save me a place.

The World Doesn't End

When it gets bad,
when my body suddenly seems too heavy
to drag out of bed
and my mind too jumbled
to pull away from my thoughts,
I remind myself of this…
The sun will still rise in the morning.
The world with all its hustle and bustle will still turn.
The clouds will clear or not and when they don't
and they pour with rain,
I will remind myself that flowers need rain to bloom.
Lakes need it to fill and maybe I need it
to wash everything away
so, on my worst days I am able to get up.
So, I can rise and get ready
because even if it's not with me,
somewhere, something good is happening
and I want to be here for that.

Unwritten

Just once, I would like to be the poem and not the poet.
Feel words written for me without having to sew them.
Have someone else say how much they've been in love,
with this person in the mirror, or the one they dream of.
Lace words just for me that feel like a poison.
Finally, be a muse for someone else to rejoice in.
Because my mind is so tired from writing these words,
filling them up with everything that hurts.
So, just one time I would like for someone else to ache,
to crumble and bend over simple mistakes.
Pour their heart out through words on a page
and create a poem for me,
one that I didn't make.

The Nature of Being Lost

I left my heart in the overgrown path
of yesterday and tomorrow.
My soul has yet,
to find its way back.

Mirror

I have loved plenty in my short life.
Things. People. Places.
Some far more than I should have.
Others far less than they deserved.
What's shocking to me
and something I hadn't prepared to learn,
was how love changes.
How it morphs into something unfamiliar each time.
Until one day you're wrapped in an embrace
that feels like home and all at once,
you've forgotten what love was.
Before this moment.
Before this person.
Everything else before, was never quite this perfect
so, it couldn't have been love then, could it?
Is the meaning of love something so fluid?
Because it seems like my definition changes
with each city.
Each smile or laugh.
Each photo or memory.
They all take me back
and somehow always mean the same thing,
the way I love life is the way it will love me.

Acknowledgments

I think writing and publishing a book has always been a dream of mine. I knew from a somewhat early age that my strength was in the way I could shape words. Still, I'm not sure I ever fully believed I could complete something like this.

I started working on this book, without knowing what it would turn into, about three years ago. Although, some of the writings do age back farther than that. However, most of my work included here was created during a time of isolation and chaos due to the covid pandemic. Assuming that many of us are alike, I'm sure no one could have fathomed just how quickly our world would be flipped upside down and jostled around. During that period and being alone for that length of time, it forced me to face myself head-on. I truly figured out a lot about who I am within these words. I did a lot of healing, a lot of reminiscing, and a lot of growing. That was all reflected in what you just read, and I have never been more proud or vulnerable in my life.

In the end though, none of this would have been possible without my small but mighty support system. To my mom, thank you for helping me push through all those late nights and doubts. To my Nina and Nonno, thank you for loving my heart and never letting me give up on these little dreams. To the ones who have been a part of my life throughout this process, you know who you are; thank you for providing me with your input and support. You will never be able to understand what that has meant to me. Lastly, to everyone who has come and gone, thank you for teaching me valuable lessons I would have never been able to achieve learning on my own.

www.ingramcontent.com/pod-product-compliance
Lightning Source LLC
La Vergne TN
LVHW100527110826
845146LV00002B/809

9798988475903